WHERE'S THE BUNNY?

BUNNY HONEY

By
Anthony Tallarico

SMITHMARK

Bunny Honey never knew so many wacky and wonderful things grew on a farm!

FIND BUNNY HONEY AT WACKY FARMS AND...

Bunny Honey likes to dance and this looks like a great party. Which costume is your favorite?

SEARCH FOR BUNNY HONEY AT THE COSTUME PARTY AND...

- ☒ Apple
- ☒ Arrow
- ☐ Balloon
- ☐ Barrel
- ☐ Basket
- ☐ Beaver
- ☐ Bells (2)
- ☐ Broom
- ☐ Cactus (2)
- ☐ Can
- ☐ Clothespin
- ☐ Coffeepot
- ☐ Crown
- ☐ Ear of corn
- ☐ Egg
- ☐ Football
- ☐ Fork
- ☐ Frog
- ☐ Headless dancer
- ☐ Hot dog
- ☐ Ice skate
- ☐ Ice-cream pop
- ☐ Jack-o'-lanterns (2)
- ☐ Kite
- ☐ Lips
- ☐ Lollipop
- ☐ Magnifying glass
- ☐ Paint bucket
- ☐ Pencils (2)
- ☐ Pizza
- ☐ Roller skates
- ☐ Saw
- ☐ Skateboards (2)
- ☐ Skull
- ☐ Snowman
- ☐ Tepee
- ☐ Train engine
- ☐ Trees (2)
- ☐ Whip
- ☐ Witch's hat
- ☐ Yellow birds (2)

Everybody loves a parade. And these bunnies can really play!

LOOK FOR BUNNY HONEY AT THE BUNNY PARADE AND...

☐ Accordion
☐ Bagpipes
☐ Banjo
☐ Birdcage
☐ Bone
☐ Boomerang
☐ Bowling ball
☐ Can
☐ Candy cane
☐ Carrots (11)
☐ Cat
☐ Chocolate bunny
☐ Clown
☐ Covered wagon
☐ Drums (3)
☐ Fire hydrant
☐ Flowerpot
☐ Football
☐ Garden hose
☐ Ghost
☐ Guitar
☐ Harp
☐ Knight
☐ Light bulbs (2)
☐ Manhole
☐ Mouse
☐ Mummy
☐ Mushroom
☐ Owl
☐ Painted eggs (12)
☐ Paper airplane
☐ Pinocchio
☐ Rocket
☐ Saw
☐ Singer
☐ Skateboards (2)
☐ Sled
☐ Snowman
☐ Spinning top
☐ Truck
☐ Turtle
☐ Whistle
☐ Xylophone

Shh...don't tell anyone. Bunny Honey is hiding in a secret egg factory.

HUNT FOR BUNNY HONEY AT THE EGG PAINTING FACTORY AND...

- ☐ Apple
- ☐ Arrow
- ☐ Banana
- ☐ Baseball bat
- ☐ Basketball
- ☐ Birdcage
- ☐ Birds (6)
- ☐ Black jellybeans (3)
- ☐ Broom
- ☐ Candle
- ☐ Carrot
- ☐ Cat
- ☐ Chimney
- ☐ Clock
- ☐ Clothespins (2)
- ☐ Dog
- ☐ Fish
- ☐ Flower
- ☐ Football player
- ☐ Knight
- ☐ Lamp
- ☐ Lost shoe
- ☐ Monster
- ☐ Net
- ☐ Other bunnies (12)
- ☐ Paintbrush
- ☐ Pencil
- ☐ Pig
- ☐ Purse
- ☐ Referee
- ☐ Roller skates (3)
- ☐ Snake
- ☐ Spear
- ☐ Top hat
- ☐ Turtle
- ☐ Umbrella
- ☐ Vacuum cleaner
- ☐ Wagon
- ☐ Worm
- ☐ Zebra

Bunny Honey is spending the weekend at his favorite bunny hotel.

FIND BUNNY HONEY AT THE HONEY BUNNY HOTEL AND...

- ☐ Balloons (3)
- ☐ Basketball
- ☐ Baskets (2)
- ☐ Bowling ball
- ☐ Burned-out light
- ☐ Cactus
- ☐ Carrots (3)
- ☐ Chef
- ☐ Crack in the egg
- ☐ Diving board
- ☐ Elephant
- ☐ Fire hydrant
- ☐ Fish
- ☐ Frog
- ☐ Ghost
- ☐ Giraffe
- ☐ Graduate
- ☐ Horse
- ☐ Jack-o'-lantern
- ☐ Kite
- ☐ Ladders (3)
- ☐ Lifeguard
- ☐ Lion
- ☐ Mouse
- ☐ Painter
- ☐ Parachute
- ☐ Periscope
- ☐ Peter Rabbit and his three sisters
- ☐ Pole vaulter
- ☐ Police officer
- ☐ Santa bunny
- ☐ Scarecrow
- ☐ Skateboard
- ☐ Snake
- ☐ Star
- ☐ Telescope
- ☐ Tennis rackets (10)
- ☐ Tree
- ☐ Watering can
- ☐ Yellow birds (4)

Bunny Honey likes to travel...but he doesn't always know where he's going!

SEARCH FOR BUNNY HONEY ON THE BUNNY TRAIL AND...

- ☐ Apple
- ☐ Arrow
- ☐ Barber pole
- ☐ Baskets (2)
- ☐ Bat
- ☐ Bell
- ☐ Bone
- ☐ Book
- ☐ Chimney
- ☐ Clock
- ☐ Crocodile
- ☐ Cup
- ☐ Curtains
- ☐ Dart board
- ☐ Dracula
- ☐ Drum
- ☐ Flowerpot
- ☐ Flying carpet
- ☐ Ghost
- ☐ Hammock
- ☐ Heart
- ☐ Helicopter
- ☐ Ice-cream cone
- ☐ Monster hands (2)
- ☐ Painted eggs (4)
- ☐ Palm tree
- ☐ Rooster
- ☐ Safety net
- ☐ Santa Claus
- ☐ Sheep
- ☐ Ship-in-a-bottle
- ☐ Sled
- ☐ Star
- ☐ Surfer
- ☐ Toaster
- ☐ Top hat
- ☐ Turtle
- ☐ Umbrella
- ☐ Wagon
- ☐ Windmill
- ☐ Wreath

Wow! What a crazy maze of daisies!

FIND BUNNY HONEY IN THIS CRAZY DAISY MAZE AND...

- ☐ Airplane
- ☐ Apple
- ☐ Arrow
- ☐ Balloon
- ☐ Baseball bat
- ☐ Basket
- ☐ Bee
- ☐ Boat
- ☐ Bone
- ☐ Camel
- ☐ Cap
- ☐ Carrot
- ☐ Clown
- ☐ Cup
- ☐ Doc Rabbit
- ☐ Elephant
- ☐ Elf
- ☐ Firefighter's helmet
- ☐ Fish (2)
- ☐ Frog
- ☐ Heart
- ☐ Helicopter
- ☐ Igloo
- ☐ Kite
- ☐ Monster
- ☐ Mushroom
- ☐ Paintbrush
- ☐ Pencil
- ☐ Quarter moon
- ☐ Ring
- ☐ Schoolbag
- ☐ Shovel
- ☐ Snail
- ☐ Snake
- ☐ Snowman
- ☐ Sock
- ☐ Squirrel
- ☐ Sunglasses
- ☐ Superbunny
- ☐ Train engine
- ☐ Turtle
- ☐ TV set
- ☐ Violin
- ☐ Watering can

Where's the bunny? Everyone is looking for Bunny Honey. Can you find him?

LOOK FOR BUNNY HONEY AT THE GREAT BUNNY SEARCH AND...

- ☐ Balloons (2)
- ☐ Baseball glove
- ☐ Bell
- ☐ Boot
- ☐ Bowling ball
- ☐ Broom
- ☐ Candles (2)
- ☐ Candy cane
- ☐ Clown
- ☐ Chef
- ☐ Dogs (3)
- ☐ Feather
- ☐ Fire hydrant
- ☐ Fishing fish
- ☐ Flowers (3)
- ☐ Frying pan
- ☐ Heart
- ☐ Hot dog
- ☐ Ice-cream cone
- ☐ Mouse
- ☐ Mummy
- ☐ Octopus
- ☐ Oil can
- ☐ Panda
- ☐ Paper airplane
- ☐ Pillow
- ☐ Pumpkin
- ☐ Reindeer
- ☐ Robot
- ☐ Sailboat
- ☐ Ship
- ☐ Skier
- ☐ Snail
- ☐ Spinning top
- ☐ Sprinkler
- ☐ Straw
- ☐ Sword
- ☐ Telescope
- ☐ Tents (2)
- ☐ Tire
- ☐ Tuba
- ☐ TV antenna

Rolling eggs on the lawn was never so much fun. Or was it?

HUNT FOR BUNNY HONEY AT THE GREAT EGG ROLL AND...

- ☐ Ant
- ☐ Balloon
- ☐ Baseball
- ☐ Bee
- ☐ Clothespin
- ☐ Dogs (2)
- ☐ Duck
- ☐ Elephant
- ☐ Feather
- ☐ Fish
- ☐ Flamingo
- ☐ Football
- ☐ Fried egg
- ☐ Frog
- ☐ Helmet
- ☐ Horse
- ☐ Jellybean
- ☐ Kangaroo
- ☐ Kite
- ☐ Magnifying glass
- ☐ Meatballs
- ☐ Other bunnies (24)
- ☐ Paintbrush
- ☐ Pear
- ☐ Pig
- ☐ Rabbit doctor
- ☐ Raccoon
- ☐ Rooster
- ☐ Scarves (2)
- ☐ Seal
- ☐ Skateboard
- ☐ Snake
- ☐ Spaceship
- ☐ Stool
- ☐ Sunglasses
- ☐ Top hat
- ☐ Toucan
- ☐ Turtle
- ☐ Walrus
- ☐ Worm

What a wacky way to run a race. Will the tortoise win by a hair?

FIND BUNNY HONEY AT THE BIG RACE AND...

- ☐ Arrows (5)
- ☐ Baby
- ☐ Barbell
- ☐ Birdcage
- ☐ Block
- ☐ Bomb
- ☐ Bone
- ☐ Cactus
- ☐ Candle
- ☐ Cat
- ☐ Christmas tree ornament
- ☐ Coat hook
- ☐ Coffee pot
- ☐ Cow
- ☐ Cowboy hats (2)
- ☐ Crown
- ☐ "DON'T STOP"
- ☐ Drum
- ☐ Firecracker
- ☐ Fishing pole
- ☐ Ghost
- ☐ Hobbyhorse
- ☐ Hot dog
- ☐ Jump rope
- ☐ Key
- ☐ Ladder
- ☐ Laundry
- ☐ Man sleeping
- ☐ Monster
- ☐ One-legged man
- ☐ Painted eggs (2)
- ☐ Periscopes (2)
- ☐ Pizza
- ☐ Sheep
- ☐ Skateboard
- ☐ Snowman
- ☐ Tepee
- ☐ Turtles (3)
- ☐ Umbrella
- ☐ Walkie-talkies (2)
- ☐ Witch's hat

A bunny's dream come true. The world's biggest carrot!

SEARCH FOR BUNNY HONEY AT MOUNT CARROT AND...

- ☐ Apple
- ☐ Balloon
- ☐ Barrel
- ☐ Baseball
- ☐ Basket
- ☐ Basketball
- ☐ Birds (3)
- ☐ Blimp
- ☐ Bunny wearing glasses
- ☐ Candy cane
- ☐ Clock
- ☐ Cup
- ☐ Diving board
- ☐ Dracula rabbit
- ☐ Flower
- ☐ Flying carpet
- ☐ Football
- ☐ Forks (2)
- ☐ Ghost
- ☐ Giraffe
- ☐ Half moon
- ☐ Jack-o'-lantern
- ☐ Kite
- ☐ Lawn mower
- ☐ Life preserver
- ☐ Lion
- ☐ Magnifying glass
- ☐ Mushroom
- ☐ Necktie
- ☐ Painted egg
- ☐ Pear
- ☐ Periscopes (2)
- ☐ Rope
- ☐ Scarecrow
- ☐ Skateboard
- ☐ Slingshot
- ☐ Snake
- ☐ "Superhop"
- ☐ Tree
- ☐ Turtle
- ☐ Whale

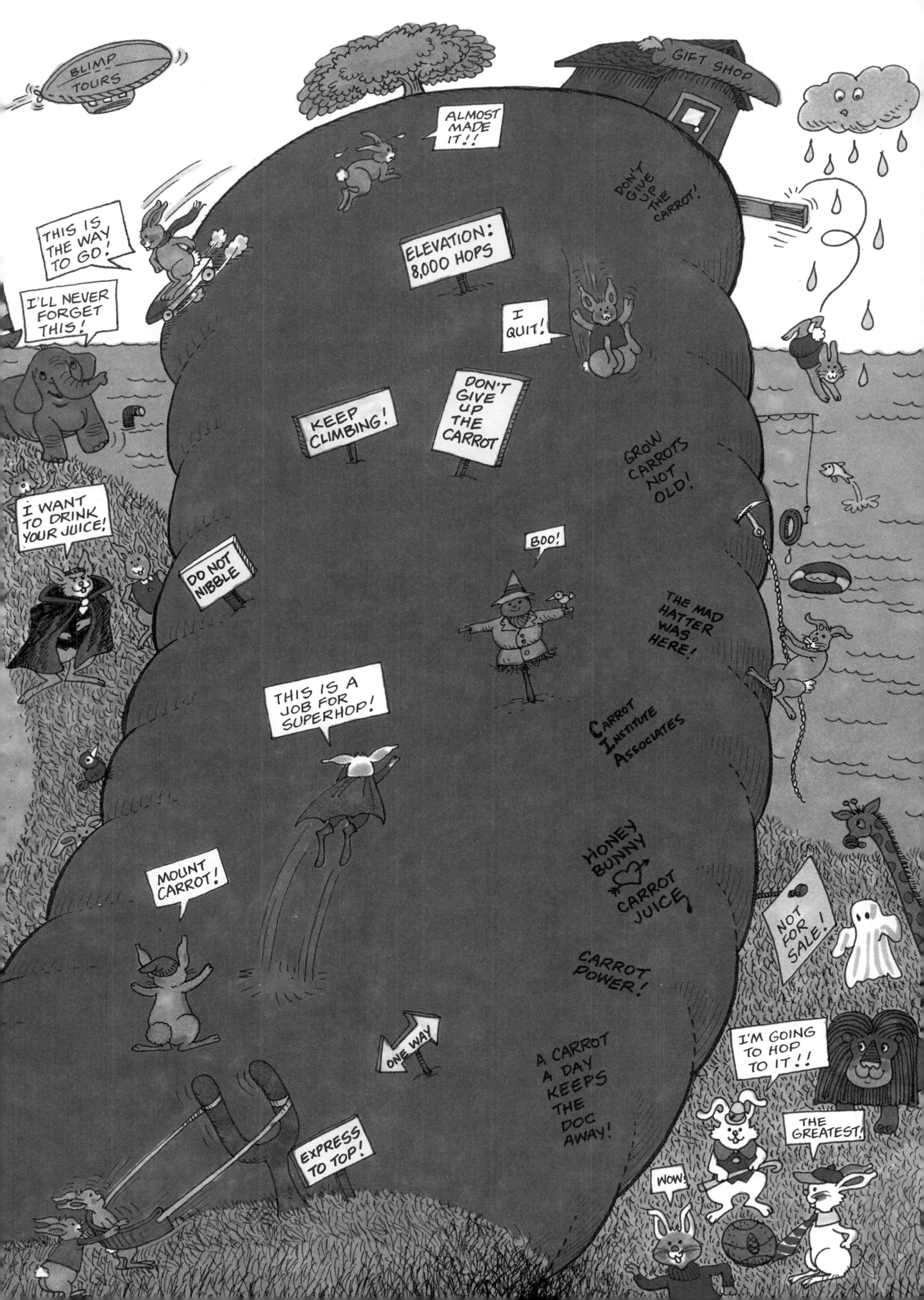

Shopping can be fun...
in a store like this!

**HUNT FOR BUNNY
HONEY AT THE
SPRING SALE
DAZE AND...**

- ☐ Arrow
- ☐ Astronaut
- ☐ Banana peel
- ☐ Basket
- ☐ Bell
- ☐ Birdcage
- ☐ "BOOT HILL"
- ☐ Boxing glove
- ☐ Cactus
- ☐ Candle
- ☐ Cash register
- ☐ Cat
- ☐ Centipede
- ☐ Chef
- ☐ Clothespin
- ☐ Clown
- ☐ Crown
- ☐ Dog
- ☐ Feather
- ☐ Fishing pole
- ☐ Flowerpot
- ☐ Ghost
- ☐ Hobbyhorse
- ☐ Horse
- ☐ Humpty Dumpty
- ☐ Igloo
- ☐ Ladder
- ☐ Lamp
- ☐ Monkey
- ☐ Mouse
- ☐ Octopus
- ☐ Owl
- ☐ Pies (2)
- ☐ Pirate
- ☐ Police officer
- ☐ Rooster
- ☐ Sailor hat
- ☐ Santa Claus
- ☐ Shopping bags (3)
- ☐ Sofa
- ☐ Sword

The jellybean planet looks like a nice place to visit. But would you want to live there?

LOOK FOR BUNNY HONEY AT THE SILLY SPACE CENTER AND...

- ☐ Apes (2)
- ☐ Baby carriage
- ☐ Broom
- ☐ Bunny costume
- ☐ Cactus
- ☐ Candle
- ☐ Car
- ☐ Clock
- ☐ Cow
- ☐ Crayon
- ☐ Doghouse
- ☐ Dogs (2)
- ☐ Eagle
- ☐ Elephant
- ☐ Firecracker
- ☐ Flower
- ☐ Fuel truck
- ☐ Giraffe
- ☐ Golf club
- ☐ Heart
- ☐ Kite
- ☐ Moose
- ☐ Oil can
- ☐ Paint bucket
- ☐ Painted egg
- ☐ Pizza
- ☐ Quicksand
- ☐ Radio
- ☐ Rowboat
- ☐ Sand castle
- ☐ Scarves (2)
- ☐ Seal
- ☐ Shark
- ☐ Shovel
- ☐ Skier
- ☐ Snake
- ☐ Snowman
- ☐ Sunglasses
- ☐ Telescope
- ☐ Ten-gallon hat
- ☐ Tricycle
- ☐ Umbrella
- ☐ Watering can
- ☐ Wrecking ball

Bunny Honey would like you to meet some of his friends.

Donald   Hector
Frankie Sam
Freddie Santa
Laura   Susie
    Lisa

WHERE'S THE BUNNY?